We Respect Our Classmates

Piper Nelid

Rosen
REAL
READERS

Rosen
Classroom™
New York

1

Today is the first day of school! Here I am with my new classmates.

This is our teacher, Ms. Howell. Ms. Howell introduces herself to the class. She tells us the rules of the classroom.

Ms. Howell says that we must **respect** our classmates. She says that we must treat each other the same way we would want to be treated.

We must respect our classmates when they speak. We must listen to what our classmates have to say.

If someone is talking, we cannot **interrupt** them. We must raise our hand if we want to speak.

Our classroom is very **diverse.** We are all **unique** individuals. We come from different places, too.

I am from the United States. My classmate, Marci is from France. Here she is holding the French flag.

Another one of my classmates is from
Japan. His name is Hideo. Ms. Howell
says we should respect the cultural
backgrounds of all our classmates.

Ben is another of my classmates. He uses a wheelchair to get around. We respect all of our classmates, no matter what our differences may be.

Ms. Howell says her classroom is a place for students to share ideas. She says we don't always have to agree with each other, but we always have to respect our classmates!

Glossary

diverse   A group of things or people that have differences.

interrupt   To stop a person from saying or doing something.

respect   To give careful thought for someone or something.

unique   Someone or something that is unlike anything else.